PLANT HOUSE

PLANT HOUSE

Beautiful spaces inspired by nature

Harper *by* Design

CONTENTS

INTRO

Synonymous with health, vitality, fertility and ancient symbolism, plants have been part of people's homes for centuries. From sharp, jagged aloe vera leaves to the curious, pea-like balls of the string of pearls, plants are living works of art, which manage to be functional and decorative at the same time. As objects of beauty, plants bring a touch of splendour to our homes. Plants are an essential part of our home's ecosystem, removing toxins from the air we breathe. Put simply, a house full of plants is a beautiful, wholesome home.

No matter your location, budget or preferences, you can create your own dream plant house. If you live in the city and crave being surrounded by nature, build an indoor jungle of potted palms, hanging ferns and some giant bird of paradise plants. If your home has limited space, you can create an innovative vertical garden on your courtyard walls to bring a slice of greenery into your life. Have a derelict rooftop in need of some love? Transform the space into cacti country with a sea of American Southwest-inspired terracotta pots filled with towering spiky wonders. Let your imagination run wild . . . your ultimate plant house will soon come to life in its own special way.

THE LIVING ROOM

The centrepiece of most homes, the living room is a real multitasker. From rowdy games nights with friends to cosy evenings watching rom–coms and chilled weekends spent reading novels in dappled afternoon sunlight, the living room is a space for all occasions. Use plants as an expression of both your individual style and your home's unique personality. One of the strengths of house plants is their supreme versatility. It doesn't matter if your pad is a modern minimalist penthouse, a 1970s–style boho beach shack or a country cottage full of charm, indoor plants will feel right at home in your living room. Want to turn your house into a home in an instant? Add a few plants and watch your living room metamorphose into a heavenly green retreat.

10

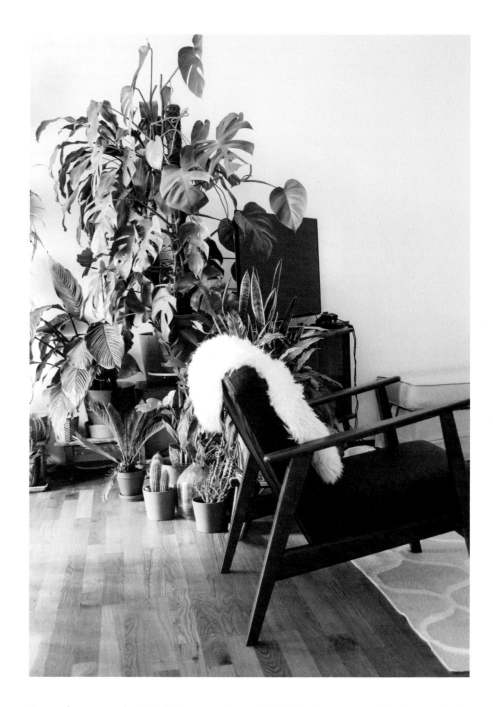

From large and stately to small and dainty, keep your indoor plant collection interesting by embracing a wide variety of species.

From stoic, sturdy succulents to wild, unpredictable vines, experiment with different plant species to bring some excitement and unpredictability to your living room.

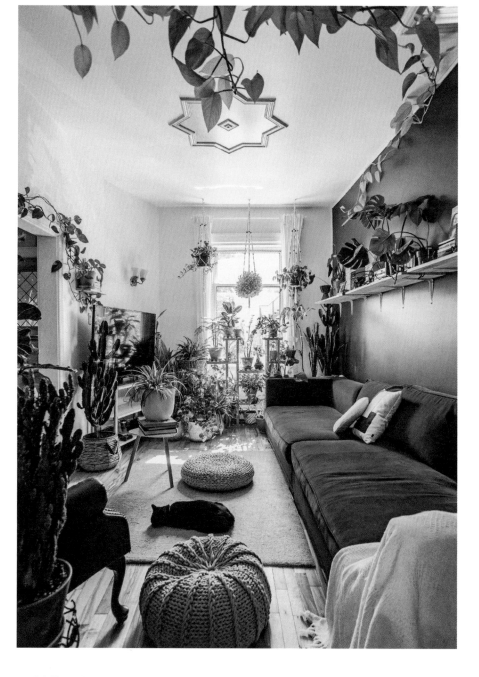

Dabbling in a range of varieties ensures your indoor jungle will have longevity. Rotate the positions of your plants to boost their chances of long-term survival.

An impressive plant collection can completely transform a space with its vibrant colour and movement.

Escape the ordinary with your very own green reading nook.

Celebrate the full spectrum of greens in nature by framing floor—to—ceiling views of lush landscapes with different species of indoor plants.

Plants with spectacular, oversized leaves are a clever way to add drama to the living room and bring life to awkward corners.

Adding greenery to both ends of this sideboard frames the statement mirror and softens the space.

A duo of emerald–green indoor plants with contrasting heights and shapes bookend this couch, adding a touch of wild beauty to the living room.

Displaying plants with pots at varying heights keeps the space visually interesting by drawing the eye to different levels throughout the room.

Carefully spacing singular plants throughout the living room offers an alternative to grouping plants together in one spot.

The striking silhouette of a solitary indoor plant
is all that's needed to bring life to this living room.

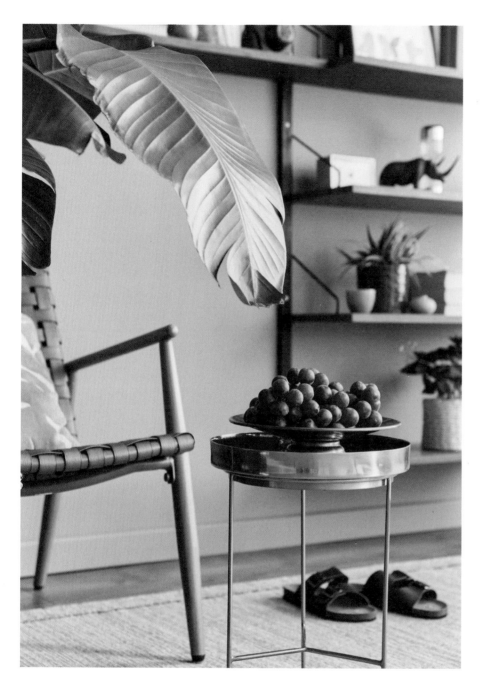

Long branches that bend around and extend over furniture
provide a comforting canopy to rest, read and daydream beneath.

Ever-changing and transformative, plants are living works of art.

No two homes are the same. Choose plant species that complement the style of your home as well as your local landscape and microclimate.

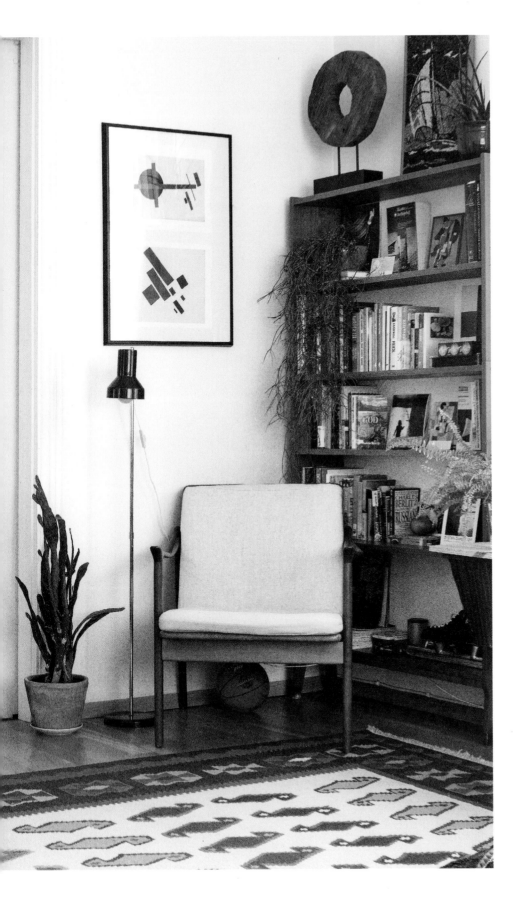

Leaves softly tumbling over a bookcase bring a sense of wildness to an otherwise static corner of the living room.

Biophilic home design increases our connection to nature.

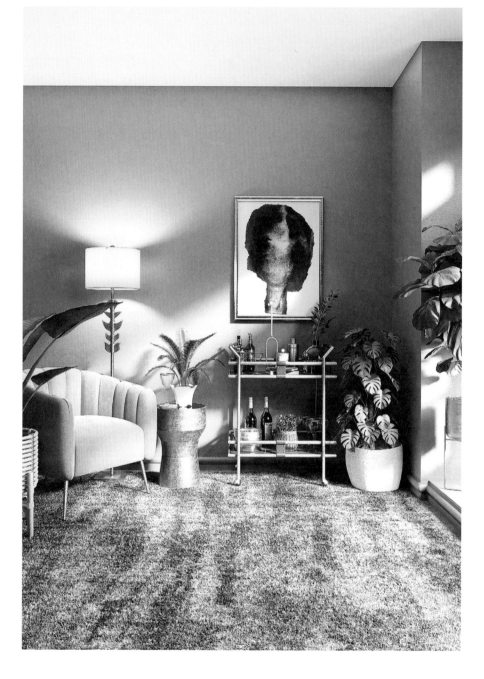

Plants can help you use colour blocking to great effect. Layering walls and floors with plants from the same colour spectrum creates a soothing, one-of-a-kind space.

The combination of stark white walls, green plants, brass watering cans and a copper velvet sofa is an inspired use of colour.

An eclectic collection of smaller plants in colourful, decorative pots is ideal for styling a small living space.

The large, imposing leaves of a monstera plant are a perfect match for a bold room filled with assorted treasures from the art and design world.

A modest selection of understated plants placed at different heights is a subtle addition to the living room.

THE STUDY

A place to do business, hit the books, catch up on life admin or lose yourself in creative projects, the ultimate study fosters an atmosphere where deep focus, lateral thinking and inspired bursts of creativity proliferate. From improved mental health to increased productivity, plants have been linked to some remarkable benefits. Tap into the superpowers of plants by infusing your study with a range of greenery. From the deep-green, glossy growth of a rubber plant to a structural snake plant reaching for the sky with its sword-like leaves, the diverse colours and shapes of the plant world will provide you with endless inspiration to accompany your work, studies, hobbies or side hustles.

Embrace plant maximalism by mixing an array of plants of different sizes and shapes in pots, hanging baskets and terrariums to create an atmospheric indoor jungle.

Placing your indoor plants near a reliable source of light ensures their healthy growth and longevity.

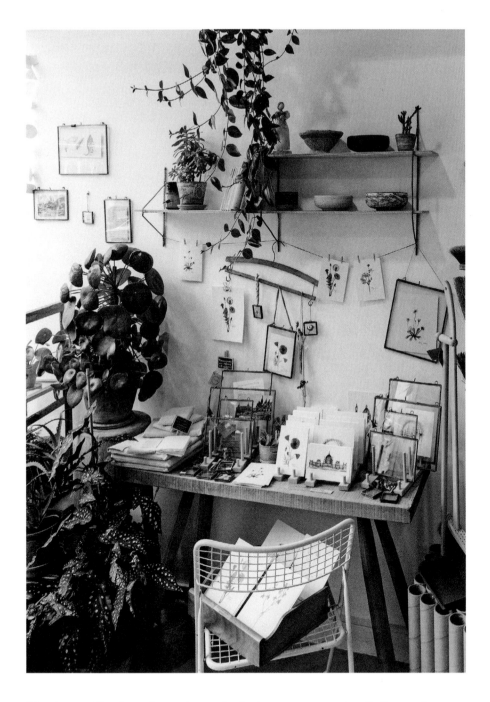

Plants purify the air and can help improve productivity and mental health. In a way, plants are the perfect study partner.

A plant-filled study is sure to brighten your mood.

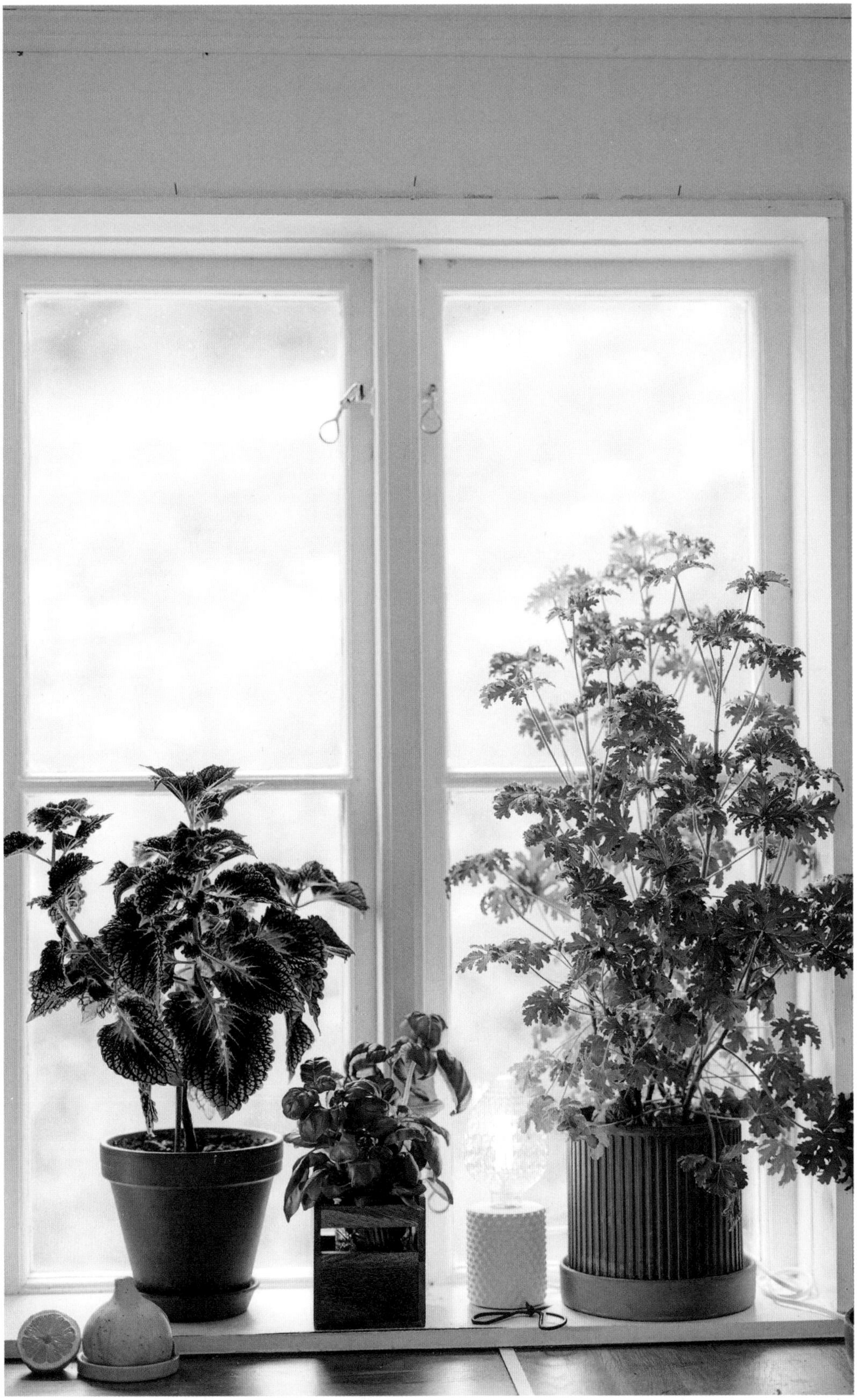

Embrace the changing seasons by arranging some foraged branches from your garden in a vase to accompany your evergreen indoor plant collection.

The Scandi–cool look of this room is enhanced
with a few select plants to frame the space.

FIRENZE
ITALIA

Calm and steadfast, plants are the ultimate work-from-home companion.

Mask imperfections and unsightly features such as electrical outlets, radiators and cords by strategically positioning plants around them.

Place a blend of hanging baskets and plants on shelves, furniture and the floor to bring character to your study space.

The emerald—green hues of indoor plants add life and colour
to an otherwise neutral space.

Use shelving to style your plant collection afresh, depending on your mood. Rotating your plants frequently ensures they all get an even amount of light.

Different plant varieties can work together in harmony.

Add some visual interest and depth to the room by playing with
height as well as leaf shape, colour and patterns like variegation.

Some plants in ornamental pots, interspersed with your favourite books, keepsakes and framed photos of loved ones, adds a personal touch to your work space.

THE BEDROOM

Your bedroom should be a calming cocoon where deep rest comes easily. Whether you live in a modern inner-city apartment, a classic country farmhouse or retro suburban bungalow, bringing plants into the bedroom is always an inspired idea. Once you've got the bedroom basics right, adding plants will enhance and personalise this special space. From a small string of pearls plant on your bedside table to a commanding fiddle leaf fig placed strategically to fill an empty corner, the options are endless. Sleep soundly knowing your plant companions are purifying the air as you snooze. Once you embrace the idea of having plants in your bedroom, you'll never look back.

Fashion a forest in your bedroom to create the illusion of sleeping outdoors. Waking up under a dreamy canopy of plant life is the perfect start to the day.

A simple timber armchair surrounded by plants bathed in sunlight creates a quiet sanctuary for reading, resting and reflecting.

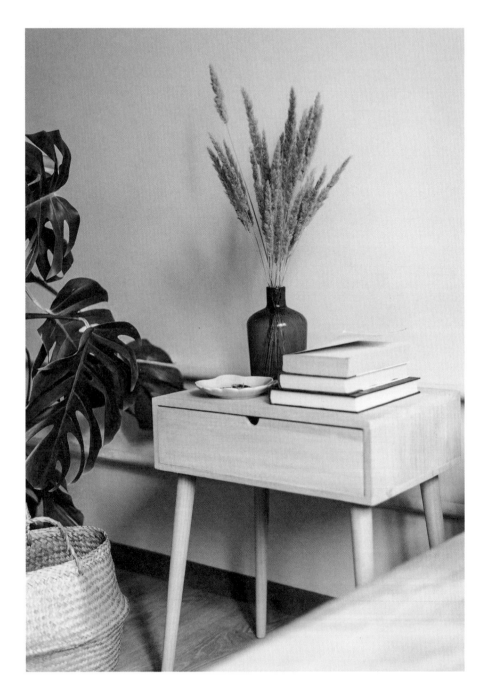

A mix of dried and living plants can be used together when styling a bedside table.

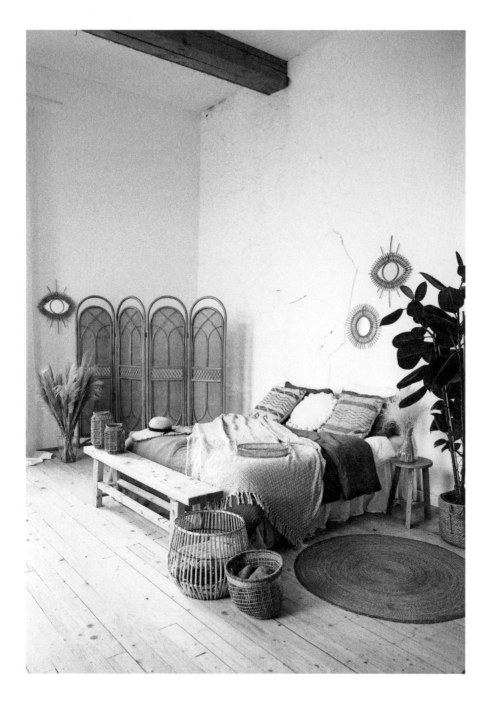

Indoor plants work well with dried arrangements and accessories
made from natural fibres, such as woven baskets and rugs.

Breathe easily while you sleep by surrounding yourself with air-purifying plants.

Framing your bed with an ethereal canopy of devil's ivy brings a hint of the wild to your bedroom. Prune it regularly to encourage fresh foliage growth.

An inventive feature wall of gold–framed hanging plants creates a cascading waterfall of jade–green foliage in the bedroom.

Placed together, a perfect pair of broad-leafed plants act as a natural screen between two spaces to create a private snooze sanctuary for guests.

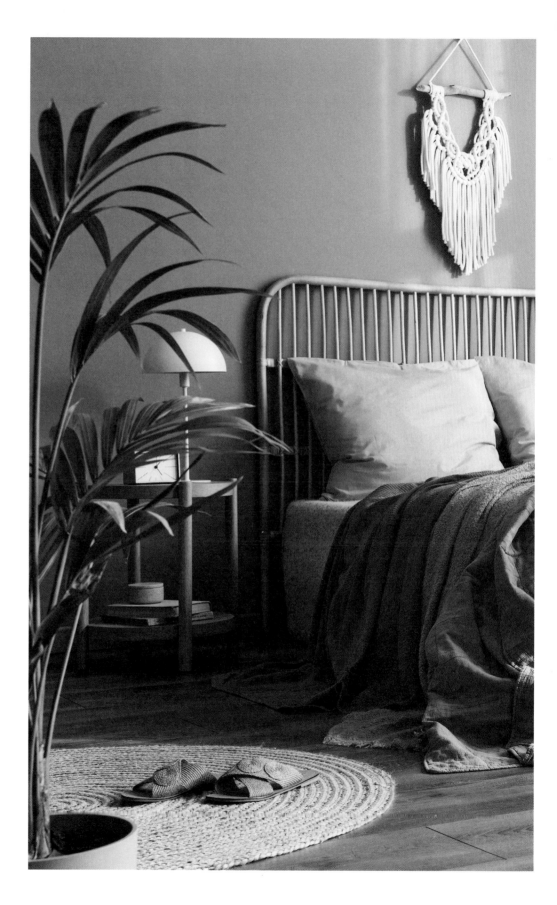

Plants inject life and colour into a room – a bright spot on an overcast day.

Embrace minimalism by using indoor plants sparingly. Just one or two of your favourite plants could be enough.

Small spaces require a restrained approach. Choose a single, hero plant in a classic basket to take the lead.

Plants cast theatrical shadows as they catch the changing light.

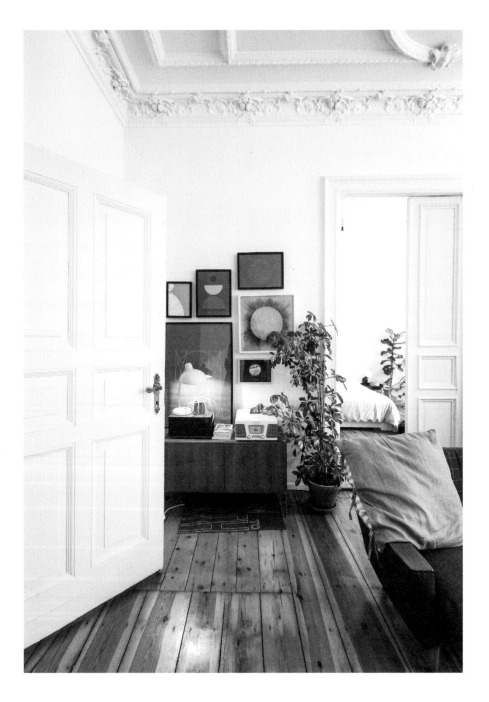

Historic homes with ornate ceilings and decorative cornices can be enlivened with the addition of a few house plants.

Just one small, elegant house plant can elevate a room that's been decorated with muted tones and a minimalist aesthetic.

Some plant varieties need streams of direct sunlight, others thrive on dappled or low light. Choose your plants wisely, depending on your local microclimate and bedroom's aspect.

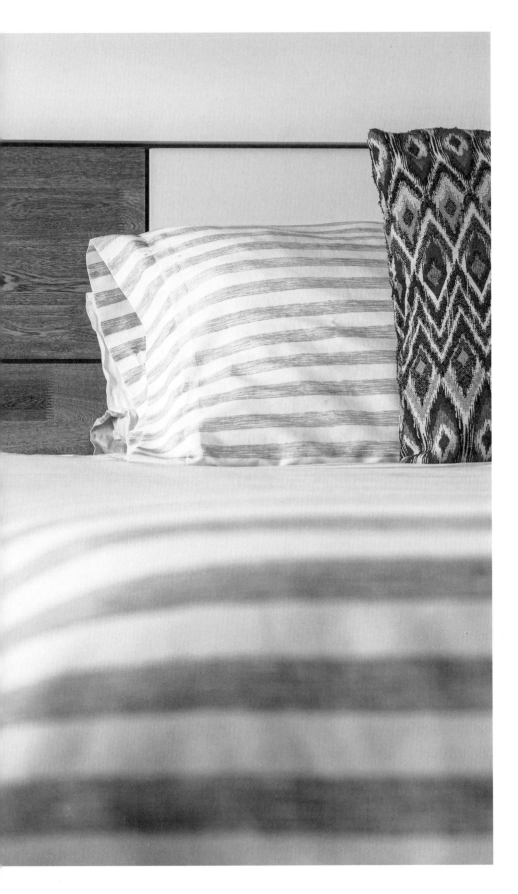

With their unlimited array of colours, shapes and textures, plants are the ultimate bedside table accessory.

A small collection of elegant plants complement, rather than overpower, a stripped–back bedroom aesthetic.

THE BATHROOM

Your bathroom is associated with purification, relaxation and wellness; plants have the power to take it from ordinary to extraordinary. The bathroom's steamy atmosphere makes it the ideal place to keep moisture–loving tropical plants that flourish in hot, humid conditions. Arrange a series of ferns beside your bathtub to recreate the bathhouse vibe or add potted palms to your walk–in shower to bring a tropical resort feel. Whether you select some small, potted philodendrons or make a statement with a huge monstera, turning your bathroom into a lush plant oasis will bring a sense of serenity and everyday luxury to your bathing rituals.

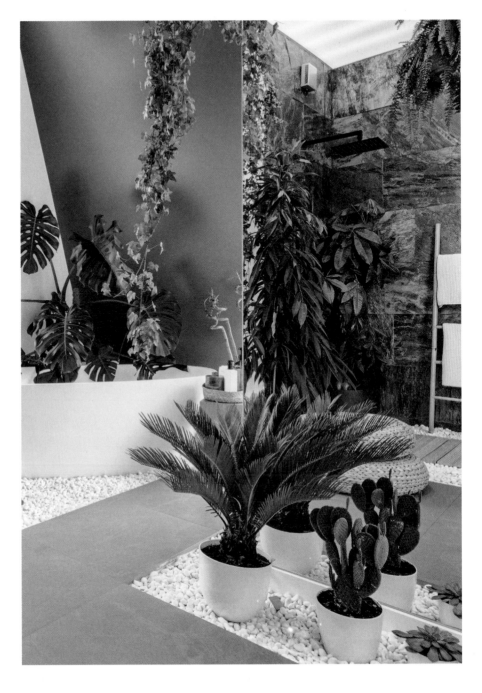

Tropical plants love humidity, so they thrive in the bathroom's steamy environment and make you feel like you're showering in a rainforest.

The combination of a deep-soaking tub and arrangement of tropical plant life transforms an inner-city apartment bathroom into a luxury resort ensuite.

Oversized, broad–leafed plants transport a bathroom
with monochromatic details into another dimension.

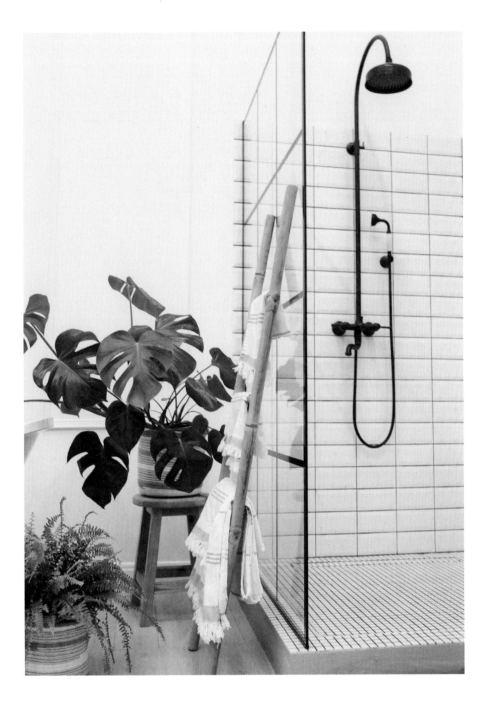

Moisture–loving plants such as ferns and monstera are well suited to the bathroom. Place them on shelves or the floor, or hang them from the ceiling — this is a room ripe for experimentation.

When it comes to the bathroom, you can never have too many plants.

With waterproof surfaces and good drainage, the bathroom is a natural fit for cultivating and caring for plants at home, especially if you lack an outdoor space.

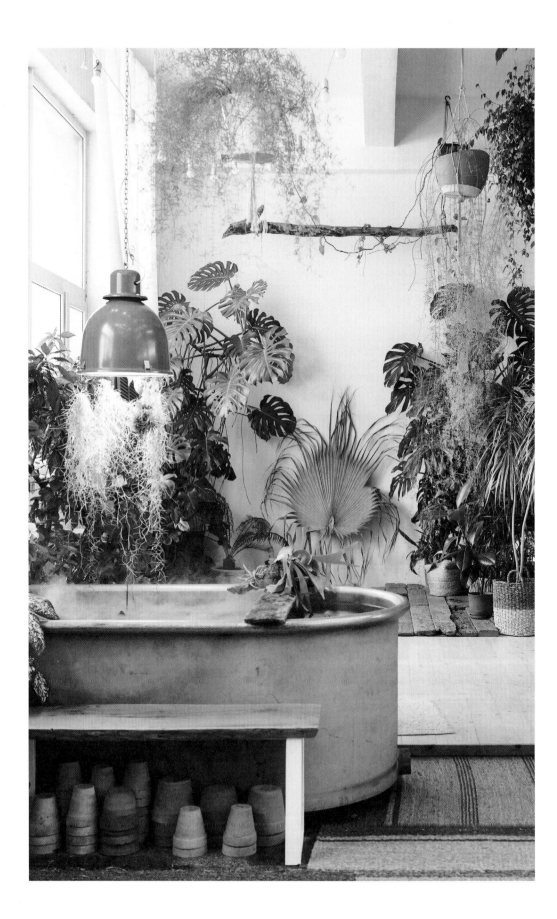

An alfresco bath surrounded by greenery takes relaxation to the next level.

Bespoke statement finishes are best matched to plants
and pots that pick up similar colours.

Grouping plants in one light–filled corner of the bathroom allows this striking copper tub to really own the space.

A tiny sculptural plant or two is the perfect addition to the clean
lines and austere walls of a minimalist bathroom.

This light and bright bathroom is enhanced by a few delicate indoor plants that don't overpower the restrained hues of the space.

Rosy tones are matched by a single plant pot. The full, bright green leaves add a contrasting pop of colour to the space without detracting from the blush–pink colour scheme.

Afternoon sun casts plants in their best light.

The ready water supply and moist atmosphere of the bathroom make it an ideal place to try your hand at propagating your own plants.

The creeping tendrils of a plant reaching out from a shelf adds dynamism to your bathroom. When placed by a bathroom window or skylight, expect your plants to grow rapidly.

Grouping plants together can have a dramatic or subtle effect, depending on the size, scale or position of your chosen plants.

THE OUTDOORS

From backyards and gardens to courtyards, terraces, decks, balconies and beyond, our home's outdoor spaces are made immeasurably better with the addition of plants. Apart from bringing wild beauty to your home, plants quietly improve and enhance your outdoor spaces in so many other ways. For plant life, providing shade, oxygen and habitat for wildlife, as well as food sources for pollinating insects like bees and butterflies, is all in a day's work. Whether you're cultivating a rooftop garden filled with colourful planter boxes, a vertical green wall of flowing ferns or a potted succulent collection on your sun–drenched balcony, plants will transform your outdoor spaces into an immersive green sanctuary. So take care of your plants, and they'll take care of you.

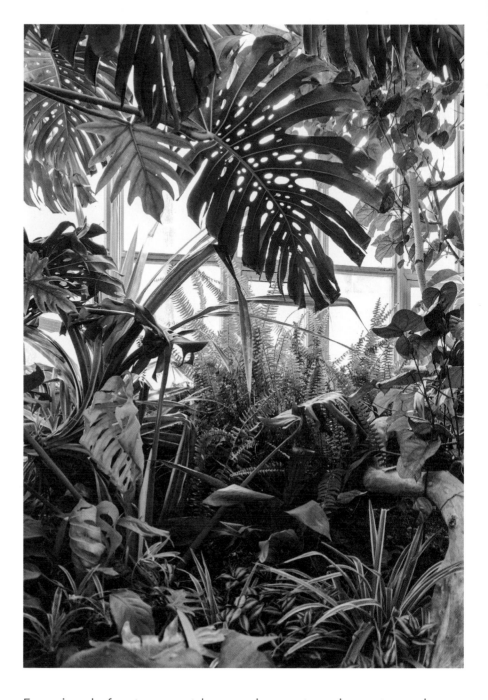

From jungle fun to an outdoor oasis, create unique atmospheres by grouping and arranging your plant collection in different ways.

Add a variety of plant life to a city rooftop or balcony to bring a touch of nature to your urban pad. String up some lights to enjoy the mini ecosystem you've created after dark.

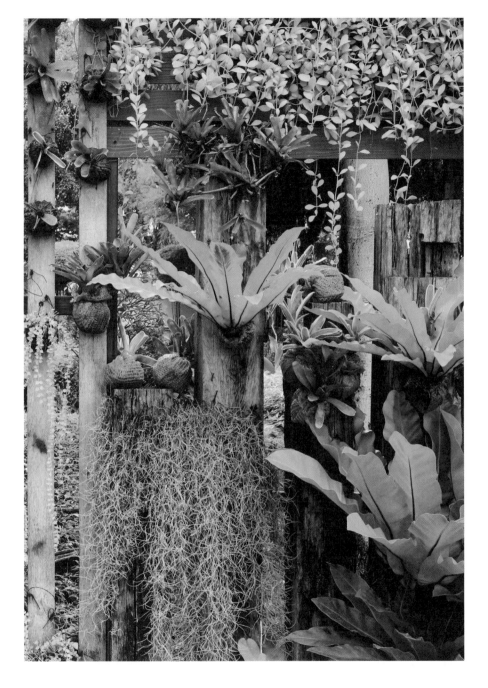

A lush living wall bursting with tropical greenery is a great idea if you're short on space or prefer a low-maintenance garden.

When working with contemporary outdoor spaces, be purposeful about where you position your plants. A few well-placed large plants will fringe a courtyard or terrace without overcrowding it.

Plants help to blur the lines between indoor and outdoor living.

Plants placed around and between chairs and at different heights create an inviting corner in a courtyard.

Cultivating a modest collection of small, hardy potted plants such as succulents is a great introduction to balcony gardening.

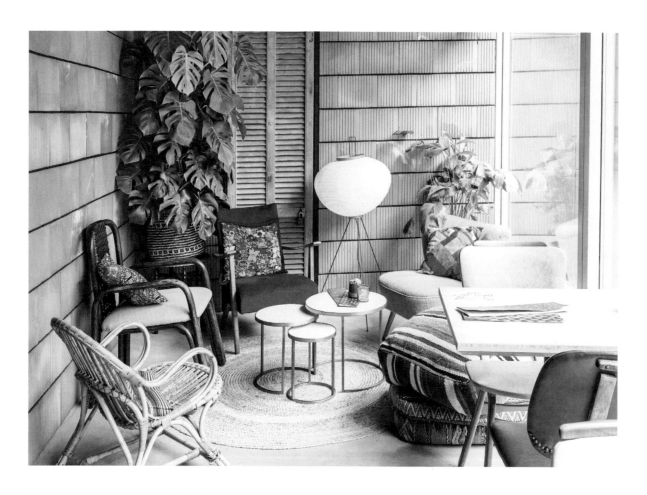

Transform an open–air dining area into an intoxicating, inviting space perfect for a lazy breakfast in the morning sun or a romantic dinner at dusk.

Make the most of precious pockets of courtyard sunshine by placing your plants where they can lap up the rays.

Use plants sparingly to enhance your favourite room.

A courtyard full of vintage, shabby–chic finds is complemented by theatrical creeping vines and palm fronds.

Hardy and structurally impressive, cacti and other succulents grow well in dry, warm climates and homes with greenhouses. They are a favourite with gardening novices.

Plant baskets hung outdoors have an otherworldly presence, like green planets suspended in the atmosphere.

Basic planter boxes made from reclaimed wood and a dash of ingenuity are all that's needed to create a low-cost, easy-care vertical garden.

Create a secret garden to lose yourself in, time and time again.

From placing potted plants along steps to using a building's exterior as a gigantic canvas, different approaches to using vertical space in gardening create vastly different results.

Create symmetrical patterns of shapes and colours on a vertical garden wall by arranging different plant species in rows.

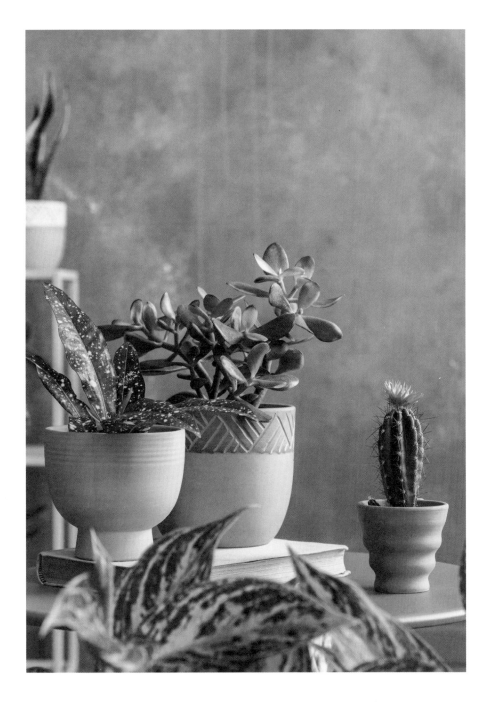

Bring some artistic expression to an outdoor space by grouping small collections of succulents together.

Let go of the idea of perfection, take a relaxed approach and let nature do its thing. The results may surprise you.

Vintage and upcycled objects such as mirrors, watering cans, bottles, jars and vases can be interspersed among your plants.

Consider different perspectives when styling your outdoor plant collection. An arrangement of potted plants takes on a new life when viewed from above.

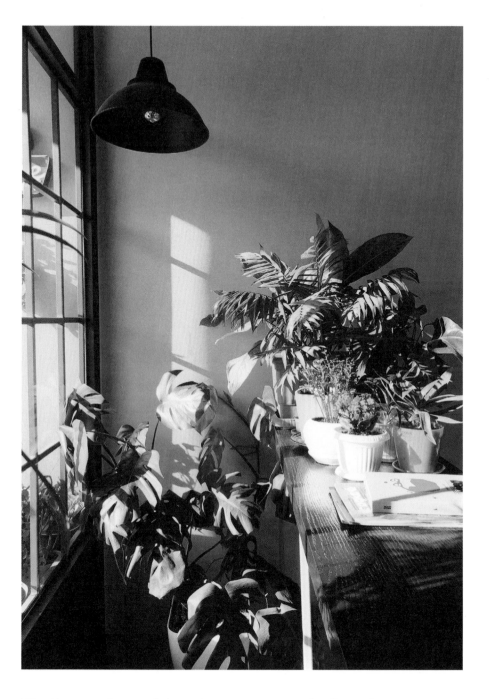

Whether you're applying greenery pragmatically to frame your home or using plants to bring beauty and vibrancy to your space, there's no right or wrong approach. Express your personality through plants and your house will always feel like home.

Harper *by* Design
An imprint of HarperCollins*Publishers*

HarperCollins*Publishers*
Australia • Brazil • Canada • France • Germany • Holland • India
Italy • Japan • Mexico • New Zealand • Poland • Spain • Sweden
Switzerland • United Kingdom • United States of America

HarperCollins acknowledges the Traditional Custodians of the land upon which we live and work,
and pays respect to Elders past and present.

First published in Australia in 2023
by HarperCollins*Publishers* Australia Pty Limited
Gadigal Country
Level 13, 201 Elizabeth Street, Sydney NSW 2000
ABN 36 009 913 517
harpercollins.com.au

Copyright © HarperCollins*Publishers* Australia Pty Limited 2023

A catalogue record for this book is available from the National Library of Australia.

ISBN 978 1 4607 6447 3

Publisher: Mark Campbell
Publishing Director: Brigitta Doyle
Editor: Jess Cox
Writer: Jo Stewart
Designer: Mietta Yans, HarperCollins Design Studio
Front cover image by Luisa Brimble / Unsplash
Back cover image by Spacejoy / Unsplash
Photographs courtesy of Unsplash, iStock and Shutterstock
Colour reproduction by Splitting Image Colour Studio, Clayton VIC
Printed and bound in China by 1010 Printing

8 7 6 5 4 3 2 1   23 24 25 26